Power to the

Poems

Turning Points into Poetic Action

by

Tamera L. Wells-Lee

Power to the Poems: Turning Points into Poetic Action © 2019

By Tamera L. Wells-Lee

Belinda,

I hope these poems will
inspire you!
God bless!
Tamara L. Wells-Lee

Message from the Author

One of the first songs I learned as a child was the "Alphabet Song," organized rhythmically around 26 letters in a style powerfully sung with commitment and conviction. That singsongy pattern would go on to inspire my own style of poetry where I write poems that rhyme with messages meant to inspire and bring about change through committed action and engagement. In that spirit, I present my first collection of poems organized around a series of positive affirmations that serve as metaphorical "turning points."

Turning points are precipitated by an ever-changing reality. These watershed moments may be brought on by experiences in our personal or professional lives, or from the pendulum of a political environment that permeates with the porosity of pouring rain. Whether drenched in sadness, overflowing with joy or steeped in retrospection, turning points provide opportunities to chart a new course toward hope and change.

This book offers reflective poems to help navigate through the reality of our times where all of us have the power to bring about change. Also included are words of encouragement and thoughtful sentiments you can share and put into action. Topics covered center around social justice, politics, equality, diversity, faith, praise, redemption, relationships, gratitude, and empowerment. I have shared my own experiences and points to consider while providing a space for self-reflection. I hope my collection of prose will guide and power you through your own turning points, enabling you to turn the tides and still the waters of life.

Tamera L. Wells-Lee

Acknowledgments

Out of nowhere words just flow
Why God has chosen me I do not know
While my poems may be too much for some
I speak from the experiences of where I come from
I mean no offense in what I have to say
When I share my reality of any given day
As an instrument, I must continue to write
To inspire, uplift, or just shed light

Although I am listed as the author on the cover of this book, I am just a ghostwriter for God. Thus, I first give Him thanks for His blessings and for using me as an instrument through the power of the poetic word. Without Him, I would not have been able to see the publishing of this book—my first collection of poems—to fruition. Along with His heavenly intervention and guidance, there have been many angels here on Earth who have helped bring this book to life.

Those include my loving and supportive husband, Kenneth, who has been a constant source of encouragement. He has been there to motivate me, and he has served as a sounding board to read, or hear me recite, my poetry. He also has inspired me through his ministering of God's Word in his role as a deacon at a Washington, DC-based church, where his homilies have messages reflective of the underlying themes covered in *Power to the Poems*. A few of those homilies are included in the back of this book as a preview to our forthcoming co-authored publication *Power to the Prayers: A Spiritual-Based Journey to Advocacy and Change.*

In addition to my husband, our daughter, Madolyn, also has been one of my biggest fans. As a Millennial, she has helped me connect my poetry to those in her age group who are part of the future of our country.

I also thank my parents, George and Ruby, for instilling in me Christian values and the knowledge and will to advocate for what is fair and just. The blessing of their upbringing, along with support from my sister, Teresa, has shaped me into the person I am today that is reflected in my poetry. Additionally, I must note that my mother was a talented writer and poet before dementia took hold of her mind. I like to think that just as God blessed her with the gift of writing, He, too, has blessed me.

There are numerous others who have been instrumental in my growth and development as a poet and a writer. They include my cousin Cynthia Turner Hicks, whose support of my poetic endeavors has spoken volumes to me in ways she may not even realize. Similarly, my sorors of Delta Sigma Theta Sorority, Incorporated have encouraged me immeasurably. While there are too many to name individually, I just want to give a special shout-out to my line sisters Stacey Crawford, Joan Demby, Darilyn Robinson, Talethia Thomas, Audra Lamb Laws, Pamela Lowry-Simms, and Carol Wynn for indulging me when I periodically flooded our group-text chats with my poems. Your sisterly thoughts, along with those of other Lambda Eta sorors, have warmed my heart.

I also thank sorors of the Washington DC Alumnae Chapter, including Nichelle Poe, who provided me with the opportunity to serve as Chapter Journalist. Serving in that capacity rekindled my love for poetry. Likewise, I am grateful for Cherie Brown Jackson for her support of my writing and for also providing me with opportunities to share my passion for the written word with our beloved sisterhood. Additionally, sincere thanks to R. Denise Everson and Laura Thalley Mayo for helping me realize and believe that this—a book of poetry—could be and is now a reality.

Finally, heartfelt appreciation to author ReShonda Tate Billingsley for her guidance and assistance with the production of this book. In thanking ReShonda, I also acknowledge her writing partner and my soror, Victoria Christopher Murray, for connecting the two of us.

Clearly, this book—*Power to the Poems*—would not have been possible without the grace and mercy of God and without the support of those who have helped me along this journey. If I did not specifically list you here, please know that it in no way diminishes my gratitude.

I am humbly appreciative. Thank you and God Bless!

Table of Contents

Introduction

The turning point where we accept change

May seem out of reach or close at range

Whatever the case, change is part of life

In good times and bad in happiness and strife

In accepting change, we may not agree to its terms

But still seek common ground and to values hold firm

Though the days ahead may bring waves of doubt

We have to go through it in order to come out

When we get to the other side of the change at hand

We will be stronger and more resilient and united in our stand

On the following pages, you will find a compilation of positive affirmations, or turning points, that serve as the basis for the reflections and poems presented in this book. The turning points are organized into four sections, much like the grouping of letters in the "Alphabet Song."

- Section 1: Anger to Gratitude

- Section 2. Hopelessness to Prayer

- Section 3. Quiet Storms to Voices

- Section 4. Whining to Zestfulness

Within each section, there are related poems meant to inspire you into action. The book concludes with journal pages to reflect on the turning points and poems. As you reflect, I encourage you to sing with power and conviction the ending of the "Alphabet Song" but change the words to *"Now I've read this poetry; I'll be the change I want to see!"*

Section 1

Anger to Gratitude

Anger to Gratitude

Anger is a fleeting but perhaps necessary emotion—necessary in the sense that anger can effect change. If the aftereffect of your anger is positive action, then you have the ability to advocate for change. **You have the ability to turn anger into action and become an agent for advocacy.** In that regard, anger can be healthy if it leads you to an outcome that is better than the situation that triggered it.

What if the outcome of that anger enabled you to literally pick up the pieces of shattered relationships and fragmented relations? Then what if you were to take those pieces and glue them together into a "bridge over troubled water" uniting people from all walks of life? Try building that bridge to a place of bonding, bypassing biases and barriers along the way. In doing so, you can **turn brokenness into bonds building bridges that bypass biases and break down barriers**. In order to break down those barriers, however, you must be committed in action.

It is one thing to be concerned but yet another to act on that concern. When you act on a concern, you show commitment. This especially is the case given the current reality of our society where some seem more inclined to work in opposition instead of in collaboration with one another for the greater good. So be concerned but be even more committed. **Turn that concern into a commitment to cultivate a culture of collaboration.**

In working collaboratively with others, much can be achieved. Take, for example, the collective power in voices united against marginalization and discrimination. To that point, discrimination of any kind should motivate you to speak out against it to lessen its impact and reach. If you have been directly or indirectly impacted by discrimination, then be determined and decisive in putting an end to it. **Turn discrimination into determination and work diligently to denounce divisiveness.**

The path you take may lead to exasperation at times, where the last thing you will want to do when you have reached your limit is talk it out or have anything to do at all with those who have offended you or the offending situation. This particularly may be the case if you believe you or others have been slighted or treated unfairly. Instead of retreating, however, realize the opportunity you have to engage in the moment constructively. Realize that you can **turn exasperation into engagement with an emphasis on equality for everyone.**

You also should realize that you can **turn frenemies into friends and find favor and fellowship with God.** By that, consider the age-old adage admonishing us to "keep our friends close and our enemies closer." However, what if you undertook a genuine effort to befriend those viewed as the enemy and put God at the core of those relationships?

With God at the center, all will be well unless you have a "sky-is-falling" mentality. If you do, then you will have difficulty seeing the goodness in people and everyday life regardless of your circumstance or happenstance. A more productive approach is to look up at what you perceive to be the falling sky and pause to give thanks for your blessings. Take a moment to **turn gloom into gratitude and glorify God for He is good.**

The Pot

Some think I'm the pot calling the kettle black.

Saying my poems are divisive, not cutting any slack.

But the stakes are high and I must go for broke.

I'm not stirring the pot but just trying to stay woke.

Poetic Justice and Peace

With all the injustices and continued outcry
I can't be silent when the stakes are high.
With calls and chants to *send her back*
People of color are under attack.
But we're here to stay as this is our home, too
Where our love for America isn't measured by our hue.
Let's stand up and make a liar out of the devil
And speak out against racism at the highest level.

The author wrote this poem to counter those who question the homeland and allegiance of people of color and our place in America.

"Write" to Press On

They say stop writing your poems 'cause you sound angry and Black
But we're still being marginalized and are under attack.
They say America will be restored and again made great
But how can that be with such divisiveness and hate?
They say we're responsible for our own racial ills
Yet they keep calling the police with privilege and at will.
They say it's not bad so stop crying the blues
But they don't know what it's like to walk in our shoes.
They say let it go 'cause we're living in the past
But I say we must press on until we are free at last!

What Do We Mean?

When we say "Black Lives Matter," what do we mean?

Should we reign above all, our rights held supreme?

Do we want the exclusionary selectivity of one race over all others?

Or do we want equality for everyone regardless of color?

While the answer to these questions may seem obvious to some,

There are those who believe we have long since overcome.

They think we live in a nation where color is inconsequential,

Saying all lives matter, race is not a differential.

While the racial divides of our past have become less of a stain;

The reality is to be Black in America means

we're still not viewed the same.

For all the progress we've made,

including a museum honoring our history;

Racism continues to proliferate, like a wound still blistery.

It's in the everyday subtleties of being overlooked and neglected.

Where on the basis of our skin color alone, not much is expected.

It's trying to vote on Election Day with our intentions at our best,

Only to realize to our detriment our votes have been suppressed.

It's in the blatant manifestation of a kill-or-be-killed mentality.

"Hands-up, don't shoot" has become our unfortunate reality.

For those who deny the daily struggles that are real to us,

Historically they have had what we seek and that's equal justice.

They haven't walked in our shoes or

seen the world through our eyes.

So they shouldn't dismiss the value

we place on our own Black lives.

When we say "Black Lives Matter,"

it's more than just the physical.

It's our thoughts, beliefs and way of being,

things not necessarily visible.

In saying "Black Lives Matter,"

it's not to exclude other hues.

Rather, it's knowing we're all created equal

and thus Black Lives Matter, too.

You Can't

You can't say you're inclusive if you leave people out.

You can't invite me to the table and then have your doubts.

You can't use me as a token to be seen and not heard.

You can't disrespect me and think I won't say a word.

You can't put me in a square because I think outside the box.

You can't encircle my mind because I have freedom of thought.

You can't "Skip to my Lou" and then skip over me.

You can't halt hate with hypocrisy.

You can't tell me to pull up my bootstraps

when you put shackles on my feet.

You can't understand my struggles when you live on easy street.

You can't see me even though my presence is right here.

You can't really know me when your vision is colored by fear.

You can't tell me what I'm feeling is not really real.

You can't define who I am and my joy you can't steal.

Our Nation Is

Our nation is divided and we must stand strong.

United as one with right over wrong.

Our nation is seeing new levels of hate.

Ignited by a firestorm to make it great.

Our nation is troubled with wounds running deep.

So watch out for those wolves clothed as sheep.

Our nation is hurting and we need to pray.

That a change is coming and we'll see a new day.

Twitterstorms

Stop with the tweets and the hate you spew.

Saying less about others and more about you.

You've got some nerve to call something a mess.

When you lack all the qualities a true leader should possess.

It's simply unbelievable that this is our new norm;

Where you create such divisiveness with your Twitterstorms.

Well, hashtag "Enough" is all I can say;

With hope for a change next Election Day!

Rise, Shine, and Vote

Rise and shine and cast your vote!

Be part of the story and not the footnote.

Be a main character in the role you portray.

And exercise your right to have a say.

Write your chapters with truth and conviction.

With outcomes based on facts not fiction.

Let your words and actions lead to a conclusion.

That it's time for a change and no more collusion.

As the plot unfolds use the power of your voice.

And be an author of a story where you have a choice.

Decree to be Free

"Oh, say can you see."

In the land of the free.

Justice for you ain't equal for me.

9-1-1, it's a travesty.

Judged by color superficially.

How can this be?

"My country 'tis of thee."

So much strife, no unity.

Oh, Father God, hear our plea.

One accord now, we do decree.

High Not Low

Don't give them the satisfaction of a reaction

other than one of peaceable transactions.

When they go low, don't come to blows;

Stay high as we know Michelle Obama told us so.

Yes, we can still take a stand;

With a purposeful plan guided by God's hand.

Even in their hate to them we can state;

Get your heart straight as salvation is never late.

Dirty Laundry

When airing dirty laundry, what do you **gain**?

Do the **tide**s change or do things remain the same?

In putting dirt out there for **all** to see,

Do you come away clean or washed in hypocrisy?

Are you **arm**ed and **hammer**ed or just ready to **bounce**?

By all the messiness of what your dirt has announced?

When cleaning up your dirt and washing things out,

Don't give folks something to gossip about.

So wash your unclean load in your own machine.

And rinse away the dirt behind the scenes.

Help clean up the dirt with a softened approach.

With cleanliness and **cheer** that's beyond reproach.

Gentrification

Gentrification is a whitewash of a people's past.

Where those who were first risk becoming last.

Displaced by the privileged who want to take over.

With no respect for their neighbors and where they walk Rover.

Well now they have come onto sacred ground.

The Mecca of where Black excellence is found.

A longstanding community that's not one to discard.

I guess they don't know who runs the yard.

Let's hope their bark is worse than their bite.

And they'll stop with this entitlement as a sense of birthright.

The author wrote this poem in response to the lack of consideration of some in walking their dogs on the campus of Howard University.

Mermaids and Sharks

Those upset because a mermaid is black;

Probably think it's okay to put some under attack.

Whereas the mermaid is fake, our reality is true;

And it's hard to believe what we're going through.

What happened to America and our melting pot?

When divisive tweets can be sent without a second thought.

And let us not forget the raids by ICE;

And the wall to be built regardless of price.

Is this what it means to make America great?

Where instead of unity some foster hate.

Just look at the "Little Mermaid" and the racial remarks;

And ask ourselves, "Are we swimming with sharks?"

The author wrote this poem to question the absurdity of those who opposed the casting of an African American as Ariel in "The Little Mermaid."

Pause

It's not a pause,
It's the end, point blank period!
First hot, then cold,
Got me feeling all delirious.
It's not imagined,
It's real, defying all logic and thought.
It could be cold outside,
But inside I'm still burning hot.
It's not right, I tell you,
To play with my emotions.
These random mood swings,
Causing all sorts of confusion and commotion.
It's no use complaining,
So put your anger on mute.
Instead, stop and thank Eve,
For she ate of the forbidden fruit!

Blessing in the Battle

Dementia devastates, divides and ravages the mind;

But there's a blessing in the battle if you only look, seek and find.

It's in the glimpses of lucidity that reminds you God is real;

It's in the gentleness of a hand stroke

that conveys the love you deeply feel.

It's in the listening and really hearing of

what your loved one has to say;

It's in the treasuring of the "present"

not necessarily the "presence" of each day.

It's in the caring of the caregiver who gives despite despair;

It's in the faith of believers who trust our burdens God will bear.

It's in the knowledge of realizing and accepting

the disease has not won;

It's in the victory of knowing God and His will to be done.

The author wrote this poem as a reflection on her mother, who has dementia, and her father, as her loving and primary caregiver.

Destination: Gratitude

Gratitude is a state with no limits or bounds.

It's a place of solace where peace can be found.

It's a destination that's reached when in fulfillment of joy.

It's stopping to give thanks no matter what life may employ.

It's yielding to the will of our merciful God above.

It's paying it forward and treating one another with love.

It's driving through the rain and basking in the sun's glow.

It's being grateful for what we have and for the blessings that flow.

Thankful

Today give thanks with hands upraised.

Humbled by His grace and joyful with praise.

Anchored in His Word that brings perfect peace.

Nourished by His love that never seems to cease.

Kneeled in prayer with gratitude to express.

Shouts of "Hallelujah" and thankful to be blessed.

Remember

Even in its rawest form, a diamond is still a precious gem.

Remember to look beyond the superficial,

for the beauty contained within.

Even during the storms, when the skies bring torrential rains.

Remember joy will come in the morning, and the sun shall shine again.

Even when we're feeling hopeless, and want to rise above the discord.

Remember there's a higher power,

and the battle is not ours but the Lord's.

Even in the bad times, when it's so hard to see the good.

Remember the ties that bind us, and love one another as we should.

Mother's Day Reflection

A mother's love is infinite, with no limit or measure;

Boundless, bountiful, blessed, to be treasured.

A compass guiding us along life's uncertain way;

A place of solace and sweet comfort come whatever may.

No judgment, just love, she's pure to the core;

A woman of strength and character, cherished and adored.

Whether celebrating yourself or giving honor to others;

Blessings to you on this day and to all our beloved mothers.

Daddy's Birthday

Husband, father, man of God.

Today and always to you I applaud.

Caregiver, provider, whatever your role.

Always your baby girl, my heart you stole.

Today is a time to celebrate you.

To thank you for all the things you do.

With respect, admiration and a daughter's love.

I wish you birthday blessings from God above.

Section 2

Hopelessness to

Prayer

Hopelessness to Prayer

When you feel like there is no hope to combat intolerance, remember that hate has no place in our current world. Know that where there is hope, there are opportunities to heal. Choose hope over hate, and **turn hopelessness into hope as a healing balm to halt hate.**

Hate also can be stopped by being inclusive instead of isolating oneself or others into silos. Isolation can come in several forms. For instance, it may be self-imposed or it could be imposed upon you. Whatever the case, aspire to be part of something beyond yourself and inspire others to do the same, especially if that something represents the diversity that defines the human race. Endeavor to **turn isolation into inclusion with an ideology that invites inclusiveness.** Doing so can bring about a state of joy and inner peace even in situations that seem unsurmountable and in perilous times.

How, you may ask, can you be jubilant about a journey that seems to be in peril? For those who believe, we know the center of our joy comes from a higher power. Thus, be joyful in simply knowing that, and **turn jeopardy into a jubilant journey of joy** even when you may be down and out.

If and when you are down for the count, lay low and take what no doubt may be a humbling experience to learn the lesson in it all. Then use that knowledge to come back stronger and equipped for success. **Turn knockdowns into knockouts kindled with knowledge**, and know you have the power to live your best life.

In living your life to its fullest, understand that it is part of a living legacy of those who came before you and those who will follow. Find joy in living and loving, and in the laughter of life, and pass that legacy on to others. **Turn life into a legacy of living, and love liberally and laugh lightheartedly**, and let go of any drama that can stifle you.

As an analogy, have you been to a play where the orchestra builds up to the climax with foreboding music? Perhaps the music foretells a story of conflict between the main characters. Then the next scene unfolds into a positive ending where the music becomes upbeat with the characters showing love and compassion toward one another. Similarly, you do not have to remain mired in the melodrama of life but instead transform it into a melody of mercy and kindness. **Turn melodrama into a melody of mercy toward all mankind.** In doing so, there will be times where you will have to drown out the noise and naysayers that may pull you back into the drama you seek to escape.

As it relates to that, a "no" from the naysayers is sometimes warranted and is in your best interest. Other times, however, it is merely self-serving on the part of those who simply do not want you to succeed. Thus, if you go through life constantly listening to those who tell you "no," then you may never realize your potential. That is why you should consider the source of the "no" and **turn naysayers into nothing more than noise and nonsense.** That mentality no doubt motivated those who have persisted and fought for justice adversity and oppression over the years.

Historically, those who have suffered from oppression have displayed resiliency and fortitude over suffering. If you have been oppressed or have witnessed it in others, then you can overcome as our ancestors and those before us did. Just like those on whose shoulders many now stand, you can **turn oppression into opportunity,** owing it to our ancestors to oppose all that offends and obstructs.

You should do that knowing that as written in Philippians 4:6, "Do not be anxious about anything, but in every situation, by prayer and petition, with thanksgiving, present your requests to God." This is one of many Bible verses that assures us that no matter the situation and even during the most difficult times, prayer works. So know that you can **turn plight into purposeful prayer.**

Hopeful

We must maintain hope in the face of despair;

Or become stagnant as people only to go nowhere.

While rhetoric and politics have divided our land;

Our call to action is clear to rise up and take a stand.

We can agree to disagree but work to benefit all;

Respecting our differences lest we perish and fall.

Look ahead with optimism and a will to effect change;

Remembering the power of prayer in God's holy name.

Diversity

Diversity is more than a singular point of view.

It is greater than yourself and not just about you.

A state of being where equality is found.

Accepting others regardless of one's background.

A conscious effort to be open and inclusive.

Breaking down barriers and being less exclusive.

A reality of a playing field that is even and fair.

Creating opportunities for all to have an equal share.

A reflection of a world where differences are embraced.

Knowing inequities and biases must be erased.

A sincere effort to rethink how your thoughts are arranged.

Putting words into action to bring about change.

Stay Woke

It's often said God knows best.

So we have to believe this is only a test.

Even if as believers we know that to be true.

It's still hard to comprehend what our nation is going through.

Let's pray we can unite in a productive discourse.

And our reality won't succumb to buyer's remorse.

There's no turning back as the path has been set.

Where some see opportunities, others see threats.

Trust in the Lord and take upon His yoke.

Knowing now more than ever we must "stay woke!"

Dream to a Nightmare

From a dream to a nightmare, that's what some would say.

"This, too, shall pass" is what we must pray.

We've seen the power behind a "yes, we can."

Keep the faith and remember how the dream began.

To be great and foster hate, is that what dreams may come?

That's the nightmare of the reality to which some have succumbed.

Although nightmares may taunt and cause quite a scare;

Just keep the dream alive and don't despair!

Common Ground

As I look ahead with hope, what do I see?

Common ground to be shared by you and me.

It's a path that unites us as the human race.

But it's a road less traveled because of the differences we face.

It's a journey to be taken hand in hand.

But it's a destination out of reach if we don't unite and take a stand.

It's a trail that paints a tapestry of God's beautiful creation.

But it's a canvas that tells the story of the "isms" in our nation.

It's a pathway we must take if we are to peacefully co-exist.

It's a trek to a place where biases we should firmly resist.

Invited to the Table

I was invited to the table and this is what I said:
"I have years of experience and didn't just get out of bed."
I surprised them with my boldness and for speaking out,
Where I emphatically stated "I know what I'm talking about."
After looks of dismay written on their face,
We had a productive discourse and reached a common place.
Although progress was made because of the words I spoke,
I will continue to advocate and no doubt stay woke.

Sincerity of Voice

You want to be a voice for our people, to help put the nation at ease.

But what do you say to those who are grumbling,

"honey chile, please"?

You want to be a soothing soliloquy offering a sweet melody.

How do you explain to others who think your motives are off-key?

You want to come to the table, willing to take the heat.

How do you respond to detractors who say you need to take two seats?

You want to bridge the divide so we're viewed one in the same.

Can that really be done when some think you only seek fame?

No one knows your heart nor your true intentions.

So we pray for you and offer up heartfelt petitions.

The author wrote this poem in response to criticisms some have faced for "coming to the table" with those on opposite sides of the political spectrum.

Redemption

When we err in judgement with results that are tragic
God's intervention is more than just magic.
It's not luck, coincidence or happenstance.
That He sees fit to give us another chance.
His grace and mercy are endlessly abound.
In Him is where redemption can be found.
Although we're flawed and fall short of His great glory
A single mistake doesn't define our life's story.
He forgives us of our sins and we need only confess.
Let go and let God and to His will say "Yes."

Bone and Flesh

Bone of his bone, flesh of his flesh.

Them two together? They've started some mess!

With just one bite, our fates were sealed.

Showing human frailties, with all sins revealed.

The legacy they've created of right versus wrong

Has become the soundtrack of our lives, our daily theme song.

When faced with a choice of good over evil

Some fall short, with actions unbelievable.

The propensity to sin is within all of us.

But God's grace is ever-present, like a compass.

Even though our beginning is defined by a single choice

We can choose to repent and thus eternally rejoice.

Waste Not Your Tears

Dry your eyes and waste not your tears
On those who dismiss you with a reign of fear.
Weep no more on what should matter the least.
Save up your reservoir and restore your peace.
When the time comes for the floodgates to flow
Be a tributary to honor those you love and know.
Dampen not your spirits on privileged passerby.
Don't let them steal your joy or a tear from your eye.

Peace Be Still

Peace be still and listen for His voice.

For in the midst of it all we still can rejoice.

He brings perfect peace even in troubling times.

Offering words of comfort to ease our minds.

He soothes our soul with a healing balm.

Whispering our names, turning sorrow into calm.

He reminds us of the sacrifice of His only son.

He assures us of the victory when our race is done.

He knows who we are and our life's story.

He reunites us in a new home joyfully in glory!

Give Thanks

If you opened your eyes to a brand-new day
Then these are the words you should pray:
"Father God, I want to thank you for keeping me;
And for your grace and mercy in which I am free.
Thank you for the blessings that continue to abound;
And for your clean heart where true love always is found.
I thank you for the rain that sometimes may fall;
For the waters that recede revealing lessons through it all.
Thank you for those who have brought out my best;
For their encouraging words through many of life's tests.
I also thank you for the enemy who brings about pain;
For in overcoming adversity I know victory is gained.
Thank you for giving me strength when I am weak;
For your eternal salvation there for all to seek.
Thank you for being true to who you say you are;
And for protecting me on my journey in life thus far."

New Year's Reflection

As you ring in the new, remember and cherish the old;

For your journey of the past is your testimony to be told.

You may have endured heartache, or suffered loss and pain;

Know joy comes in the morning with the sun rising above the rain.

In bidding farewell to last year and celebrating the new;

Rejoice in overcoming the battles you've been through.

Take delight in your joys and celebrate your success;

Giving glory and honor to God, trusting He knows what's best.

Go forth with hope for opportunities that abound;

Reflect on your past from which your tomorrow can be found.

Prayerful Change

Woke up this morning to a new day of hate
With the loss of more lives to make America great.
Let's unite in love and pray for those affected
With prayers for our nation to what we're being subjected.
A message of peace has to come from the top
With a sincere call for unity and the hatred to stop.
We all can be the example we want to see
With prayers for change as our hopeful plea.

Action Item

It is often said that we should pray

But prayer without action means issues will stay.

While we must still call on our God above

Specific steps are needed to turn hate into love.

I don't have the answers on what should be done

But know action is needed to end violence with guns.

When Someone Is

When someone is broken, bless.

When someone is empty, enrich.

When someone is falling, fortify.

When someone is hurting, help.

When someone is longing, love.

When someone is neglected, nurture.

When someone is rejected, restore.

When someone is pained, pray.

When someone is suffering, sympathize.

When someone is wandering, welcome.

On any given day, that "someone" could be any one of us.
So be compassionate and be a blessing to others.

Hope in Christ

Christ has risen according to God's word!

Through His death and resurrection our sins He incurred.

We need only to confess, accept and believe

That eternal life after death can be achieved.

From Heaven above victory is won.

Let's celebrate the blessing of His risen son!

Breaker Breaker 1-9

Breaker Breaker 1-9, what's your 10-36?

I'm resting peacefully with our Lord, in His presence I'm transfixed.

I'm over in glory where the streets are paved with gold;

10-4, Hallelujah, my name's been written on the Holy roll.

Breaker Breaker 1-9, my journey has been a long haul;

But my Father in Heaven has been my guide, with me through it all.

He's here with me now and my soul is at eternal peace;

And he's there with you, too, to help bid your sorrows cease.

Breaker Breaker 1-9, I've driven in sunshine and rain;

But praise God Almighty I'm now healed and no longer in pain.

To my family and friends, in time your eyes will be dried;

10-4, over and out, until we meet again on the other side.

The author wrote this poem in memory of her uncle,
a long-haul truck driver who passed away November 2016.

Section 3

Quiet Storms to

Voices

Quiet Storms to Voices

The song "God is Trying to Tell You Something" is a reminder that we often need to take the time to listen for His guidance. Further, as Psalm 46:10 tells us, we need to "Be still, and know that He is God." Seek those quiet moments to reach that inner peace. When you do so and truly submit to the will of God, you can **turn quiet storms into quests for quiet time with the Lord**, even during those times when the rain pours.

Those rainy seasons are a part of life, literally and metaphorically. Without the rain, light would not be able to reflect off the rainwater to form beautiful rainbows. Without the rain, we would not be able to replenish our physical and spiritual dwellings. So soak up the rain and welcome the growth ahead. **Turn rainstorms into rainbows that radiate with rebirth and renewal.** In that season of rebirth, know that you can break the chains that have been holding you back.

Those chains, or shackles, can be of the physical and mental sense and are meant to shame and control. In spite of that, shackles cannot take away your freedom of thought. With that freedom to think, you can use those shackles to succeed. You can **turn shackles into springboards and soar to success.**

You also can overcome turmoil, as turmoil does not have to equate to defeat. Rather, it can force you to dig deep to rise above the chaos and pain. It can show you what is possible in improbable situations if you just trust that victory is attainable. In trusting, you can **turn turmoil into triumph over trials and tribulations**.

Some may describe the current climate in which we live as a time of great trials and tribulations, or as being in a state of unrest where there is dissension along political, racial, religious, socioeconomic, and gender lines. You can accept that or seek God, who has dominion over all and who can unite us as one. You can **turn unrest into unity, unbreakable and united under God**. You can use the power of your voice and combine that with others to accomplish that.

Collectively, our voices are stronger and invoke a feeling of "yes, we can." Consider this and know that in whatever manner you choose or are able to communicate, you have the power to speak out against injustices and for the least among us. You have the power to **turn your voice into voices and vehicles to vanquish vices that victimize and violate the voiceless**.

God's Light

Though trials and tribulations seem to cloud your day
God's love will shine light along your life's way.
His light can heal, His light can soothe.
His light has the power to make mountains move.
God shines His light in the darkest of hours.
Illuminating His love, strength, and heavenly powers.
A source of comfort and tranquility, bringing perfect peace.
His light is a healing balm, bidding your sorrows cease.
Providing a compass through the storm to a home over in glory.
Lighting a pathway to His kingdom to shout and tell your story.
His light shines bright and remains forever lit.
A reminder of His compassion lest we slumber and forget.
No matter your pain, struggles, loss or plight
Seek the warmth, love, and comfort of God's perpetual light.

Conqueror

Whether it's the perfect storm or a domino effect

This, too, shall pass for it's only a test.

Find strength in those with wisdom to impart

And trust in the Lord with all of your heart.

Lean not on your own but understand this to be true

The battle is not yours for He will see you through.

Look with hope beyond your current sorrow

Joy comes in the morning and the sun shall rise tomorrow.

Whatever your trial, tribulation, happenstance, or fear

You are more than a conqueror and victory is near.

God's Marvel

Pause and marvel at what God can do.

As the world bore witness in the Thailand cave rescue.

He was the oxygen in the tanks supplying their every need.

God true to form and abundantly to exceed.

He was with the divers giving them strength to swim.

A light bringing hope even when things seemed grim.

He reigns supreme as protector of us all.

There to pick us up and answering our prayerful calls.

The author wrote this poem following the rescue of a youth soccer team trapped in Thailand caves during the summer of 2018.

Leadership

Built on a legacy of answering the call,

Where our leadership in action helps sustain us all.

We have a servant's heart and a passion to lead,

With a desire to ensure we'll continue to succeed.

We often find ourselves in a leadership stead,

With vision and forethought as we think ahead.

We're humble in our service and face adversity with grace.

We know leadership is not always about winning the race.

We have a purpose and a calling to uphold the legacy of our past.

We will continue our leadership journey and shall remain steadfast.

The author wrote this poem to reaffirm her own personal commitment and philosophy to servant leadership both personally and professionally.

The Magic of Making History

Magical moments can be happenstance
or cultivated over time;
Celebrated inconspicuously or
with the grandeur of heights divine.
They can be here in the present or
preserved throughout the years;
Recognizing our small triumphs or
conquering our greatest fears.
They can result in cultural shifts and
alter what seems unconquerable;
Juxtaposing the stagnation of progress
with forces that are unstoppable.
They can represent our adversities but
with a deep resolve to overcome;
Symbolizing an ending over suffering because
glory to God we did not succumb.
They can capture humanity at its lowest but
with our spirits still flying high;
Giving birth to new movements for
in vain our ancestors did not toil and die.
They can be illustrative of the light
guiding us during our darkest hours;
Shining a spotlight on our successes
while we give thanks to a higher power.

They are our flashes of brilliance and
purposeful plans on display;
Building upon a legacy before us,
we make history each and every day.

Politics Over People

When politics trump the people, the reality is such a shame.

Because the least among us suffer and become pawns in a game.

It's like when all the bases are loaded and the innings are running late.

They fail to close it out when stepping up to home plate.

When it's fourth and goal with the playoffs on the line

They can't convert the play and the clock runs out of time.

With Game 6 of the finals and a deficit to surmount

They act like it's a scrimmage where the outcome doesn't count.

When attempting to restart play with a kick of the ball

They fail to score a goal and are blocked by a defensive wall.

When playing roulette where the wheel spins and spins

They drop the ball on us and no one really wins.

Our lives are not a game and the consequences are real.

Put people over politics and work to reach a deal.

The author wrote this poem during the threat of a shutdown of the federal government of the United States.

Reality Check

If we're all "created equal" as originally declared and conceived

Then how can we make that a reality, a legacy to be achieved?

Is our reality hooded by the rule of Three-Fifths?

Where along racial lines there are still many deep-seated rifts.

A reality manifested into the light of each new day.

Where leaders among us have given life for hate to have a say.

Where the history of one's heritage has created cultural divides.

Where love for all mankind is in conflict with one's own self-pride.

Where love for thy neighbor has been the exception not the norm.

Where we're shrouded by differences fueling inconceivable firestorms.

A reality that came home to the architect of our nation's birth.

A gathering of those who view others as a fraction of their worth.

A reality where we must unite and declare "This is not right!"

Acknowledging the symbols of our past

in the context of our current plight.

A reality where we can choose to do right or perish in doing wrong.

Where we can create a legacy of equality, one nation united and strong!

The author wrote this poem in the days leading up to the August 2017 Unite the Right rally in Charlottesville, Va., near where the author was born and reared.

Black and "Mis-ing"

Words, misstated.

Stereotypes, promulgated.

Actions, misinterpreted.

Lives, short-circuited.

Ideas, misappropriated.

Thoughts, disassociated.

Voices, misrepresented.

Injustices, unprecedented.

Protests, misconstrued.

Contexts, confused.

Justice, misaligned.

Black, undermined.

Emergency

9-1-1, it's an emergency.

I woke up this morning black as can be!

I want to go outside but don't know what I'll face.

'Cause some think it's a crime simply because of my race.

Get in my car and drive downtown?

Will I be pulled over and stopped for driving while brown?

Go to the park and fire up my grill?

Will I be able to relax, hang out, and just altogether chill?

Go jump in the pool on a hot summer's day?

Will the supremacists among us let hate have a say?

Go to work and be recognized for what I do?

Will I be dismissed by those of a different hue?

9-1-1, it's an emergency.

End racism now and pray for unity.

Freedom

It's the Fourth of July and freedom 'tis so sweet.

But lest not forget our beginning with shackles on our feet.

Ripped from the womb of our Motherland.

Beyond all comprehension, hard to understand.

Brought to a nation pursuing its liberty.

Declaring in 1776 that America was free?

But emancipation for us was nowhere in sight.

Not even years later on that star-spangled night.

Auctioned off, sold, and treated worse than cattle.

Did the Civil War really put an end to that battle?

In spite of our founding, we have risen above.

For it's His blood-stained banner we hold up in love.

Celebrate the Fourth, but know this to be true.

God endowed on us the freedom we all are due.

"Some" of Our Reality

Some say all lives matter but I ask "what about us?"

When we're back to those days of sitting in the rear of the bus.

Some say we're no longer separate but instead viewed as equal.

Why are Black lives being lost like an insufferable sequel?

Some say they're pure in heart with love for all mankind.

Why do we still live in a nation where love and hate are intertwined?

Some say the problem is on us, with brothers killing brothers.

Why is that flawed logic used to justify the actions of others?

Some say we're ungrateful and disrespect the signs of democracy.

Why can't we have the freedom to protest

when those symbols are shaded by hypocrisy?

Some say justice is fair and to everyone it's evenly applied.

Why are some not held accountable for their connivance and lies?

Some say we foster divisiveness and

"Black Lives Matter" is urban blight.

But we're not the "some" of our reality,

where we still seek our God-given rights.

Tokens

Are tokens only tokens if they don't know they've been taken?

Could any semblance of reconciliation be otherwise mistaken?

How can we have a seat at the table without being shut out?

How can we help facilitate change without being viewed as sellouts?

I don't purport to have the answers but these questions I do pose,

During these troubling times where the pendulum continues to flow.

We must remain cautious, astute, engaged, and informed,

And identify ways to constructively weather the storm.

Uncle Ben

Oh, Uncle Ben, like rice you're getting sticky.

To call slaves "immigrants"? Now that's more than a little tricky.

What happened to your brilliance, the man with the gifted hands?

Because this here lunacy is so hard to understand.

Just stop for a minute and take all of this in.

Would your "immigrant" ancestors still claim you as their kin?

It's okay for us to disagree and have different schools of thought.

But don't make light of our ancestors and the battles they fought.

You see, the Middle Passage was not one that they willingly took.

In shackles and chains is not a trip anyone would want to book.

So get your point across without distorting the facts.

Because misspoken words have power and from the real issues distract.

The author wrote this poem in response to a prominent public official
who referred to slaves as immigrants.

Double Negative

If you believe the "double negative" and never-ending froth

Then I'm positive you're cut from the same sheep's cloth.

Though we all misspeak and our tongues get tied

There's a difference between the truth and an outright lie!

Promised Land

He went to the mountaintop and saw God's great glory.

Knowing it wasn't the end but the beginning of his life's story.

He caught a glimpse of his Dream and what dreams may come.

Knowing the totality of his life was greater than its sum.

He marched without fear to whatever fate may befall.

Knowing he was a drum major for justice and equality for all.

He's "woke" even in death with the years that have passed.

Knowing the promised land is near if we just remain steadfast.

Right is Wrong

"Unite the Right" is in-your-face hate
With false promises of making America great.
Supremacy for some to the exclusion of the whole
Is not a mark of greatness but of the evil in one's soul.
They seek purity of race with unclean hearts
With privileged ignorance mistaken for smarts.
In uniting the right, know this to be true
They are wrong and misguided in the hate they spew.

Reserve Your Judgement

I'm quiet and reserved; I sit back and observe
But don't underestimate what I can do.
I don't have to be loud, or stand out in a crowd
To prove I'm as qualified as you.
I can know what I know without having to show
How I got to where I am today.
I can be me even though you can't see
Beyond what your stereotypes portray.

Step Into Your Destiny

Step into your destiny and know your worth.

This is your season for a time of rebirth.

The past is the past and a new day has come.

The adversity you've faced is not the total of your sum.

Look at our God showing up in grand style.

Guiding you to success and triumph over trials.

Continue to be faithful and surrender to His will.

Just trust and believe that your dreams will be fulfilled!

Section 4
Whining to
Zestfulness

Whining to Zestfulness

Face the reality. Life can be hard and it is easy to get caught up in our own pity party. When you are in the midst of crying a river, it may be hard to see the positive and turn that pity party into a party with a purpose. Remember, however, that the source of your complaints also may be a cause for celebration in that your lows may ignite within you a winning spirit to achieve new highs. So strive to **turn whining into winning and do not wallow in the waters of weariness**. This includes when you are consumed by fear of or a dislike for others.

When you are in that all-consuming space, you should know that it usually takes a lot of wasted energy to hate someone on the basis of that person simply being different. Instead of fear or hatred of others, try instead to be hospitable. Try to **turn xenophobia into xenial relationships**. Let go of any hate or pain so you can free yourself to live your destiny.

In letting go, ask yourself if you are living your best life and if you are fulfilling your dreams and pursuing your calling. If you are not, then you are holding yourself back from a destiny that is within your reach. Instead, **turn yourself into the you that you are destined to be**.

In fulfilling your destiny, there will be some folks in your ear ready with a biting comment. Do not give them the satisfaction of deflating your spirit into a ball of nothingness. Instead, resolve to be positive and rise above to new heights. **Turn zingers into a zest to go from zero to a zillion.**

When He Looks at Me

When he looks at me, he sees nothing else
But a small portion of my true self.
When he looks at me, I see confusion on his face
The lack of understanding of another people's race.
When he looks at me, his dislike is clear
With biases and stereotypes based on ungrounded fear.
When he looks at me, I look back
With wonderment of the love and compassion he lacks.
When he looks at me, I do not respond with hate
Refusing to accept intolerance and racism as simply our fate.
When he looks at me, I must maintain my presence of mind
And show love and respect for all mankind.
When he looks at me, I have a responsibility to bear
To peacefully protest even in the face of despair.
When he looks at me, he conjures up the bloodstained past
Triggering incomprehensible actions, no questions asked.
When he looks at me, I have to prove my life's worth
Justifying the value bestowed on me by virtue of my birth.
When he looks at me, he fails to see we are the same
Created equal by God, spoken into existence by His name.
When he looks at me, I pray and I pray
For a colorblind people in this world today.

Can We Get Along?

For those who espouse intolerance and hate

Stop and ask, "Can I get through Heaven's pearly gates?"

Think before you speak and to your own sins first confess.

Treat one another with love then let God do the rest.

Take a stance in whatever form or fashion.

Regardless of beliefs, maintain respect and compassion.

And don't pontificate over right versus wrong.

Instead stop and ask, "Can we all just get along?"

United in Victory

Conservative? Liberal? Whatever the case may be.

Can we treat one another with dignity?

Our views may be different but at the end of the day;

It's not us but God who will have the final say.

So what do we gain with all this discord?

If we live a life that's not pleasing to the Lord?

Let's come together now and unite as one.

Knowing through Him, with Him, in Him victory is won.

Cultivate Change

A culture of complaining doesn't cultivate change.

So plow a path to positivity that's within your range.

Prune your whining so you can focus on success.

Plant seeds of winning and prepare to be blessed.

Make your bed for flowers to bloom.

Welcome the sunshine to brighten the gloom.

Coloring Book

As children we draw with colorful crayons.
We see the beauty of each hue reflecting me and you,
creating pictures showing the diversity of life.
We paint the world through innocent eyes
not blinded by racism, classism and other "isms"
that cause colors to quickly fade to black and white.
Then we learn to write with pencils
words that convey our thoughts
and begin to define our existence.
Words characterizing who we are
but of which others can erase
and consider mistakes with no questions asked.
Pencils transform into pens
that lend themselves to
a sense of permanency and relevancy.
After all, the pen is mightier than the sword
until the ink bleeds, smears suppressing and oppressing.
Pens become pings of technology
as game changers for capturing, disseminating
and globally sharing an ever-growing divide
between the haves and have-nots.
They create race-based misconceptions and disunity
with the very colors once viewed as a luxurious tapestry
illustrating how harmonious and peaceful life can be.

Can we go back to basics where it's okay to be different

and valued in a collection with different colors?

Where it's okay to color outside the lines and cross borders

and live and love regardless of pigment with no limit?

Can life be like a child with a coloring book?

Where there's beauty in the variety of how we all look?

Love Always Wins

Magi crossed the border into an unknown land
Welcoming the birth of our Lord, the Savior of man.
Guided by the light of the star above
To see Christ Jesus who would go on to preach love.
Love for thy neighbor regardless of race
Compassion for all and for the struggles some face.
With Mary and Joseph, to Egypt He fled
To escape evilness and impending bloodshed.
His birth brings hope in the midst of it all
Breaking down barriers when some want to build walls.
While the circumstances now are different from then
The moral of the story is love always will win.

Choices and Change

I can have love for my country but still show concern

When bridges of unity continue to be burned.

I can honor those who've fought valiantly for our great U.S.A.

But I cannot remain silent for the voiceless who have no say.

I can kneel and be prayerful or stand and salute.

It's a freedom of choice on which we must not become mute.

I can be a spectator in life where the stakes are high.

Or "fired up, ready to go" can be my rallying cry.

I can love my neighbor even though we may disagree

Rising up to unite against hate and bigotry.

I can do what is comfortable or do what is right

With joyful change in the morning, even after the darkest night.

Election Results

They marched to remove the shackles from our feet

Evoking a spirit of winning and not one of defeat.

Setting out on a path to free us from oppression

Advocating for equality and contesting suppression.

Sacrificing their all to give us the right to choose

Fighting for a privilege we should not misuse.

Overcoming adversity and remaining steadfast

Reminding us of why our votes we must cast.

Reflecting on those who have paved the way

We are called to action on Election Day.

Confused Times

No quid pro quo and no collusion?

These are troubling times with so much confusion.

The left thinks it's right yet the right is left with wrong.

Both sides divided and unable to get along.

Is this just a side effect of our democracy?

With abuses of power and such hypocrisy.

Are there moments from the past with lessons to teach?

As the question remains of whether to impeach.

Do we accept what is without having a say?

Or do we vote for change next Election Day?

Vote for Change

The results are in and the people are tired

Saying "out with the old, you are fired!"

At one time elected to serve the people

Trying to steal our democracy and all but the church steeple

Well there was a vote for change on this Election Day

That served as a reminder of having our say

Like an "apprentice" let us learn and adhere

And vote for more change in November next year

The author wrote this poem mostly in response to Election Day 2019 results in Virginia and Kentucky.

Let Go

Let go of the hurt.

Let go of the pain.

Let go of the guilt.

Let go of the shame.

Let go of the baggage.

Let go of the weight.

Let go of the bitterness.

Let go of the hate.

Let go of the sadness.

Let go of the stress.

Let go of the chaos.

Let go of the mess.

Let go of the damaged.

Let go of the flawed.

Let go of the haters.

Let go and let God.

A Year in Your Life

What does a year mean to you?

Is it only your past or the future you're going to?

Do you reflect and learn on life's ups and downs?

Do you look ahead with hope for opportunities to be found?

Do you accept "what is" or help do what is best?

Do you share your testimony of how you've endured the test?

Do you forgive and forget as we fall short and are flawed?

Do you trust His holy will and let go and let God?

Do you see the blessings even in the storms that have passed?

Do you welcome the new year while giving thanks for the last?

In reflecting on what this year has meant to you

Remember to cherish the old as you ring in the new!

Victory in the New Year

On the occasion of celebrating a brand-new year
Seize the moment to give thanks and reflect on all you hold dear.
While the past has been filled with highs and lows
Just remember from Him all blessings abundantly flow.
With passion and purpose as you prepare to start anew
Claim the victory God has waiting especially for you!

Graduate to Something New

When I first held you, I graduated to a new realm of being
Where my love became immeasurable and motherhood was freeing.
Free to love with no limits and cast my worries to God
Standing firmly beside you without pretense or facade.
I've watched you grow and blossom into the you you've become
Not bowing to pressure but marching to the beat of your own drum.
As you graduate and move on to life's next stage
Know the sky is the limit as you come of age.
With the freedom of thought and to love with free will
You have boundless potential for your dreams to be fulfilled.
Be true to yourself like the purity of my love for you
And take each day as a blessing of something bountiful and new.

Removing Self-Doubt

Self-doubt prevents you from being who you're meant to be.

An obstacle along your life's path, a detour from your destiny.

It's easy to take a backseat and watch life pass you by.

Stilled by a soft-spoken voice, not knowing when to amplify.

Don't let your quiet reserve silence who you truly are.

More than a whisper or an inanimate avatar.

You're who you are with tremendous potential to succeed.

Have faith and believe God will supply your every need.

Don't let fear cause your confidence to deflate.

Rise with self-assurance for the opportunities that await.

Can I?

Can I live and be Black without being attacked
because God made me a different hue?
Can I be treated the same without having to proclaim
that I have the same rights as you?
Can I know what I know without having to show
the value of my life's true worth?
Can I speak of the wrongs without sounding headstrong
when all I want is peace on earth?
Can I breathe and be me without denying I'm free
when I seek all the freedoms I'm endowed?
Can I express love of oneself without hatred for all else
when I shout "I'm Black and I'm proud"?

Speak It

Speak it into existence and claim it to be.

Go out and make it happen and fulfill your destiny.

It may seem impossible to achieve your goals.

But put your faith in God knowing He is in control.

Go ahead and say what God has planned for you.

And prepare for the blessings of your dreams coming true.

Jesus Joy

"Jesus joy" has got me grinning.

In Him I can shout "I'm winning!"

A smile on my face and praises to sing

I'm ready for whatever today may bring!

Season of Blessings

Your time has not passed as it has yet to come.

For this season of your life is not the total of your sum.

You may have experienced highs and the lowest of lows.

But where God is leading you is for Him to know.

Even at your peak with a future that seems bright.

He can redirect your path if the timing is not right.

Listen and be obedient when He wants you to be still.

Trust in His holy name and surrender to His will.

With God in control, there is no need to second-guess.

So prepare for your season to be abundantly blessed.

Time to Shine

I was told it's a cop-out to write poems that rhyme.

So I asked myself, "Why am I wasting my time?"

I guess I had no business writing this book.

'Cause that critique I got just left me all "shook."

But there are those who like the cadence of my words.

Saying my poems are inspiring and need to be heard.

So while some may not like this style of mine.

I've written my book and now watch me shine!

About the Author

Tamera L. Wells-Lee hails from outside Charlottesville, Virginia, and has resided in the Washington, DC area for most of her adult life. She has worked in the publishing industry for nearly 30 years, where she has held positions such as Managing Editor and Director of Publishing for publishers geared toward the academic, library, legal, and trade markets. Although Tamera has worked in publishing for a number of years, she has not had the opportunity to publish her own book until the publication of *Power to the Poems*, her first book of poetry.

As an aspiring poet, she has performed her poetry as part of Open

Mic Night at Busboys & Poets in Washington, DC. Additionally, she has penned several poems for and about her beloved sorority. She has a bachelor's degree in communication from Old Dominion University and a master's degree in business from The Johns Hopkins University.

Tamera has been married for 24 years where she has been the "fire" to her husband's "ice." She and her husband are the proud parents of a daughter who is in her third year of college.

To stay in touch with Tamera and for information on book signings and other developments, visit her website at www.tamerawellslee.com.

"Power to the Prayers" Preview

Coming soon...

Power to the Prayers:

A Spiritual-Based Journey to Advocacy and Change

by Deacon Kenneth Lee and Tamera L. Wells-Lee

<u>Excerpt from Forthcoming New Book</u>

Isaiah 1:17 tells us, "Learn to do right; seek justice. Defend the oppressed. Take up the cause of the fatherless; plead the case of the widow." Further, in Psalm 145:18 we are reminded, "The Lord is near to all who call on Him, to all who call on Him in truth." These verses are the essence of living a life of service to others, advocating for those in need, and how prayer is central to all we do. In living a prayer-filled life where the Lord is ever-willing to hear our petitions and our praise, Scripture is the perennial guide along our life's journey that enables us to advocate and bring about positive change.

On the following pages are reflections that speak to what God has called us to do and of His enduring love, grace, and mercy.

Do We Hear the Call?

Isaiah 6:1-2a, 3-8; 1 Corinthians 15:1-11; and Luke 5:1-11

by Deacon Kenneth Lee

Do we hear the call? Jesus calls people to follow Him, and we also recognize that He is calling us. The call of the Lord comes in many ways—through dramatic inner visions as in the call of Isaiah or through the simple actions that we hear in the Gospel Luke 5:1-11, which are still miraculous, or through the preaching of others as we hear in Saint Paul's First Letter to the Corinthians. The call of God to His people is persistent and perennial.

Calls are powerful in animals and humans. Within the monastery, monks discern calls, too, and understand that the most awesome call is the one from God.

The Prophet Isaiah describes how God touched his mouth. The call of this prophet begins with a heavenly liturgy. It is not clear whether this is an inner vision of Isaiah or a strong dream or some other way of perceiving the reality. On the other hand, it is clear that Isaiah takes it as God reaching into his personal life and cleansing him so that he can proclaim God's word to others. Because of this awareness of being cleansed and purified, Isaiah feels that he can be a mouthpiece to be sent by the Lord to His people.

We can note three things about this Divine call—(1) it comes from God; (2) there is a purification and cleansing; and (3) finally, there is a willingness on the part of the one who is called to respond with assent.

Saint Paul in his First Letter to the Corinthians speaks about his personal call to serve the Lord. It also comes directly from God (even knocking him to the ground!); it purifies him (making him aware of God's plans in a way he had never thought of before); and Paul becomes willing to follow the Lord. To this is added, "For I am the least of the apostles, not fit to be called an apostle, because I persecuted the church of God. But by the grace of God I am what I am, and His grace to me has not been ineffective."

We can sometimes feel unworthy of the call from God, but that's okay. When a person becomes keenly aware of his utter dependence on God, his unworthiness, and God's infinite mercy, he is on a holy path to a greater intimacy with the source of his life. God called and continues to call some unworthy characters: King David, Mary Magdalene, the penitent thief at Our Lord's Crucifixion, Dismas, you, and me. Doesn't this give us all hope for our salvation, the ultimate reunion with God the Father? Or do we doubt the call?

Do we hear the call? Peter doubts the words of Jesus commanding him to drop his nets, but, nonetheless does Jesus' bidding. It is because Peter obeys that he discovers the presence of God, is humbled, and then follows Jesus. James and John seem to display little resistance to the call of Our Lord.

We are called by our baptism to follow the Lord. We are purified, regularly if we only confess to our sins. And, yes, we will have doubts. But, in obedience to the Word, we can encounter the Living God.

Jesus, who lives in the Church and in the world forever, is calling us into deep waters to be fishermen.

Do we hear the call?

Are We Totally Committed?

1 Kings 17:10-16; Hebrews 9:24-28; and Mark 12:38-44

by Deacon Kenneth Lee

Are we totally committed? Let us take a moment to let that sink into our spirit as we examine closely the Gospel of Mark 12:38-44. In those passages, we see people in the forefront of religious activity who practice giving the appearance that they are holy and righteous, totally committed to God. As we all know too well, appearances are not all what they seem. The scribes are the so-called religious ones who do not give a very good example of those who are totally committed. They are learned men who know the Word but who do not live the Word. However, we have someone less learned in the religious ways who gives herself totally to the Lord. You see, the scribes viewed religion as a success route that is similar to the corporate ladder.

They liked to go around in long robes, using their prayer shawl outside of prayer time as a showy and flashy way of displaying for all to see their so-called piety. They would accept ceremonial bows from the people as a mark of respect for their alleged superiority. They made it a point to place themselves before the people in the synagogues, taking a seat on the dais at banquets, and made their prayers long. Jesus adds that they devoured and stole from the widow.

Widows are a Bible favorite. Widows were looked upon as a powerless and unprotected class, having to stretch and save their resources carefully. The widow we see in the Gospel here had little to give, but she put in two small coins. She gave quietly from a loving heart. She was not well learned in the religious matters of the day, but she knew God better than the scribes. She was totally committed. She could have made a good case for not being in the position to contribute anything at all. Or she could have put in one of the coins and kept the other. However, this widow knew that true giving must have sacrifice connected with it…maybe even a certain courageous recklessness.

Too often the rich expect to be celebrated and commemorated for their giving. The poor on the other hand, when they let their hearts be touched and share what little they have, often expect nothing in return. The widow's faith meant a great deal to her. She was not casual about it, and her commitment to it called forth generosity of spirit. Jesus said she put in more than all the other contributors.

So what should we take away from these stories and circle back to the question posed at the beginning? The widows teach us that goodness is not confined to the people who profess to be religious. Indeed, we can all appreciate the words of Shakespeare that any work, kindness and mercy "is twice blessed: it blesses him that gives and him that takes."

Are we totally committed? True religion is not about putting on a show proving how much you know. True religion is about inspiring new heights and depths and breaths of goodness as generosity, altruism, and compassion, as with the widow in the Temple. For certainly, the true practice of religion helps further motivate good people to their best selves and to practice love's self-giving.

We are beautifully imperfect and we must continually ask for God's mercy and grace to face our difficulties—at work, within our family, and in our community—with religious faith, courage, and generosity. Let us try to be a giver rather than a taker, to help and not hinder, to build up and not tear down, to encourage and not to criticize, to be thoughtful and kind, a ready listener to the troubles of others, and be motivated by the genuine caring taught and exemplified by the good Lord of our religion.

Be *totally committed,* and be blessed.

What is in Your Heart?

Isaiah 35:4-7A; James 2:1-5; and Mark 7:31-34

by Deacon Kenneth Lee

What is in your heart? My brothers and sisters in Christ, the above-listed Scripture readings offer us hope and encouragement. We are His beloved in how He has blessed us and given us a new hope, by healing us from our afflictions, our sicknesses and shortcomings. God has promised and fulfilled the promise He made to make us whole again. Why? Because He created us out of love.

The prophet Isaiah spoke about the coming of God's healing to His people as the signs He would show when He sent His Savior into the world. The prophet Isaiah was sent to the people of Israel at the time when many in Israel had abandoned the Lord and His ways, and they suffered at the hands of their enemies, scattered and exiled away from their homeland.

Isaiah spoke of a new hope for the people of Israel, who were surely downtrodden and despairing, remembering the time of their suffering in Egypt when they were enslaved by the Pharaoh and the Egyptians for hundreds of years. They longed for the coming of the Deliverer, whom the Lord has promised for many years through His prophets and messengers that deliverance would come for them.

109

The prophet Isaiah spoke of the signs of what would happen when the Messiah of God came into the world. He would make the blind people see again, the deaf people to be able to hear again, the mute people to be able to speak again, the lame and the paralytic to be able to walk and to be active again. And all of these would happen as signs of the coming of the one whom God has promised to us.

And echoed in the Gospel of Mark 7:31-34, we hear the moment when the Lord Jesus healed a man who was both deaf and mute. He touched his ears and mouth and by His words, "Ephphata!" (meaning "Be opened!") the Lord healed the deaf and mute man, who could immediately hear and speak once again. The man praised the Lord and the people who witnessed the great miracle also were astonished and glorified God. It would be safe to say they definitely had joy in their hearts.

What is in your heart? Rest assured, it was the fulfillment of what God himself has promised to His people, that through His Savior that He would restore His people from all their afflictions and disabilities, from all of their shortcomings, pains, and sufferings. It was through the Lord Jesus that the plan of Salvation was completed to its perfect fulfillment. But it was not all the physical healing of the people that were the focus of Christ's objective in this world, but rather, the healing of our true and deepest sickness that has made us all to be sick.

Time and again we have "fallen into shadow," to borrow a phrase from the Lord of the Rings. What am I referring to, my brothers and sisters in Christ? I am referring to the sickness caused by our sins. Sin is caused by our disobedience and refusal to obey God, which afflicts each and every one of us, ever since Adam and Eve, our first ancestors, were tempted and failed to resist the temptations of Satan, to disobey God's will and commands.

Ever since then, we have been dealing with sin, which is truly a disease and corruption upon our entire being. Sin is the disease that affects first the soul, and then from the soul, to the heart and mind, and eventually our physical self and the whole body will be affected as well. We may be physically healthy and untouched by any physical diseases or sicknesses, but in truth, deep inside us, we are sick and dying because of this sickness of our sins.

What is in your heart? And unlike all other physical diseases and sicknesses, which can be cured or halted to a certain extent by medicines and treatments, there is no cure for sin except for the Lord's mercy and grace alone. None but the Lord is capable of forgiving our sins, and no one but the Lord is able to free us from bondage to our sins.

What is the meaning of all this to us, my brothers and sisters in Christ? Every single one of us as Christians, who have been baptized in the Name of the Lord, have gone through the rite of the Sacrament of Baptism, we experienced the miracle recalling the precise moment mentioned in the Gospel passage cited here, when the Lord Jesus opened the ears and loosened the tongue of the deaf and mute man, proclaiming, "Be opened!"

And more still, that through the holy water of baptism, all of us have been made to be sharers and partakers of God's New and Everlasting Covenant, which He has made with all of us through the action of His Son, Jesus Christ, Our Lord and Savior. By that water of baptism, we have been cleansed of our past sins and our original sins, and we have been purified from our wickedness and unworthiness.

111

What is in your heart? Therefore, as all of us have received the inheritance from God of faith, hope, and love—by sharing in the death of His Son, Jesus Christ, on the cross dying for our past sins—and now having shared in the hope of the glorious resurrection from the dead that He has shown us, each and every one of us as Christians have been called to be active in our faith, to be the ones to bear the Lord's truth to all the peoples of all the nations. Cultivating confidence that morning by morning we can awaken with a conscious appreciation of life, giving God thanks in prayer for our existence that day by day, we can make a conscious effort to live our lives in such a way that we reflect the goodness of the Savior and that evening by evening, we can wind down our daily activities with calm resolve that we have made a positive impact in the lives that we have encountered.

Our Christian faith is one that requires us to be active, to be missionaries and to reach out to others about the faith we have in God. We cannot be complacent or inactive and passive in the practice of our faith. We have been freed from the tyranny of sin and death, and the veil of sin has been lifted up from us. We have experienced God himself being present in us. So what is stopping us from truly proclaiming the Lord in our lives?

Remember the Gospel is opened to the poor and the rich alike, the powerful and the powerless, the humbled and the proud. Let us be open and attuned in the ways of Christ to the needs of those in our midst, wherever we find them or ourselves.

Let us therefore strive to be true disciples of Christ, truly living up to our calling as those whom the Lord has chosen out of the world, having been given the truth and the promise of eternal life. Let us go forth and preach this truth to many more people, through our words, our deeds, and our actions, that in everything we say and do, we will always proclaim the glory of God and call many more to come to the Lord and be saved.

Let what is *in your heart* always reflect the love of God. Be encouraged and be blessed.

Are We Good Enough?

Deuteronomy 30:10-14; Colossians 1:15-20; and Luke 10:25-37

by Deacon Kenneth Lee

Are we good enough? The Scriptures cited here challenge us about what we know and what we think we know. They tell us that those who obey the commandments will be rewarded with prosperity. However, the prophets condemned those who were wealthy for they often took advantage of the poor and had lavish lifestyles without giving consideration to those who were needy or struggling. How true then as it is true now.

We are reminded that there are more precious things in life than having big stashes of wealth. The author of the Book of Wisdom prayed for prudence and the spirit of Wisdom and stated all gold, in view of her Wisdom, is little sand and before her silver is to be accounted even less. In the same way, Plato even agrees in his teachings in *The Republic*, where he states that "true riches come with a good and prudent life as opposed to the counterfeit treasures of gold."

Are we good enough? Now what is one to do? You see the apostles were thinking of the idea in Deuteronomy that those who obey God's commandments will be rewarded with prosperity. But Jesus had a different view: "How hard it will be for those who have wealth to enter the Kingdom of God?" Then He goes on to say that entering the

115

Kingdom is not easy for any of us. He tells us, "Children, how hard is it to enter the Kingdom of God?" Jesus' example of a camel getting through the eye of the needle was to illustrate graphically that it is not possible. However, it is possible with God's grace: "For human beings it is impossible, but not for God. All things are possible for God."

Jesus' response after the rich young man left was in disappointed surprise. He saw that the rich man, whom Jesus saw with love, would prefer worldly wealth to the riches of the Kingdom of God. Sometimes those who have wealth, even a modest amount, feel they are condemned when they hear the Gospel referenced here. No, brothers and sisters, that is not the case. Let us first realize that early missionaries, such as Saint Paul, would have had greater difficulty in founding churches in various cities and towns without the help of those who were wealthy. The early churches had to gather somewhere to hear God's word and to celebrate the Eucharist and that was usually at the home of someone of means whose place was large enough to accommodate everyone. This was because church buildings did not exist until the 4th century.

Are we good enough? Keep in mind that Jesus has a cautious view about wealth: "Where your treasure is there will your heart be." (Matthew 6:21) Any of us could be led astray by wealth, no matter how much we may have or not have, if we lose our focus on God's kingdom than on what is really our worth. In another example, He tells us about the story of the sower and the seed. Remember the seed that fell among the weeds and as it tried to grow it got choked out? Jesus compared those "who hear the Word, but the cares of the world, and the lure of wealth, and the desire for other things come in and choke the Word and it yields nothing." (Mark 4:19). In this context, even the poorest among us can be so absorbed by activities and distractions such as television, cell phones, music, sports, the Internet, and the list can go on and on. We end up making no time for prayer, or to come to church, or live as Christ has taught us.

Your "one thing more" may not be to "sell what you have and give to the poor" (Mark 10:21). It might be:

- forgiving;
- loving an enemy;
- admitting an addiction and taking it to the Lord;
- repenting;
- starting evangelization;
- tithing;
- saying "yes" to a particular vocation, and
- engaging more in your church and local community.

At this moment, Jesus is looking at us with love. Give Him the "one thing more." Give Him all your love and know *you are good enough.*

Don't Be Afraid

Baruch 5:1-9; Philippians 1:4-6, 8-11; and Luke 3:1-6

by Deacon Kenneth Lee

Don't Be Afraid. Are you afraid of the dark? God wants us to enter into a dark place during the season of Advent. That is what the practice of penance is about: putting aside our usual self-denial and entering into the dark places in our conscience. In those places, we hide our knowledge of the sins we have done and the good we have failed to do. In that darkness, Christ can appear as light if we are willing to allow Him entrance.

The beginning of Gospel of Luke 3:1-6 puts Saint John the Baptist's ministry in its worldly context by spelling out what sort of men governed the world into which the Messiah was born. The leaders were corrupt. This is why Saint Luke mentions them, so that we understand that John—and Jesus after him—faced uphill battles.

Don't Be Afraid. Our faith is challenged daily. Through news channels, the Internet, and social media we absorb sometimes horrid news about pain, suffering, and death. We wonder, "Where is God?" Abject poverty, terrorism, hate crimes, and abuses of all forms shake our faith. We persevere in His Advent, our faith hard-wearing. Despite these terrible setbacks and disappointments and losses, early Christians acknowledged, and modern-day Christians reaffirm His call to the light of His Glory.

119

Saint John the Baptist "went about the entire region of the Jordan proclaiming a baptism of repentance which led to the forgiveness of sins." This might strike us as a rather holy endeavor. But imagine if John were to appear on your own doorstep. It is likely that you would want nothing to do with him, perhaps because of his appearance, but even more likely because of his words. He tells everyone without exception how it is. People like him do not win popularity contests. Fortunately for all of us, entrance into Heaven is not based on popularity but fidelity.

When Saint John the Baptist speaks of sinners, he points out their sins. Yet when he speaks of Christ, he points and shouts, "Behold, the Lamb of God who takes away the sins of the world."

It is important for us to realize the significance of both of the directions in which Saint John is pointing. He points to our sins so that we see the darkness inside us caused by our sins. But he does not stop there. After pointing to our sinfulness, John points to the Lamb of God so that we might see the light of Christ and in Him know forgiveness, reconciliation, and peace—real peace and not the peace offered by the world.

Don't Be Afraid. It is not safe to think or act like Saint John the Baptist, of course. But if our love is to abound more and more, we must be willing to embrace those whom we do not care for or even consider as part of God's plans. We need to recall that we ourselves were once far from the Lord and that He "has done great things for us."

Take a very common example of sacrifice to reflect on what God calls us to during Advent. There are a lot of different sacrifices that parents are called to make to prepare for their unborn child. Parents have to be ready to sacrifice space; for example, to figure out where the child is going to sleep. Parents have to be ready to sacrifice money, of course, lots of money for all sorts of needs.

Parents also have to be ready to sacrifice some of their favorite vices. They have to be ready to become less selfish and more selfless. The problem for all of us is that the longer we cling to our vices, the more entrenched those vices become in our lives and the harder they become to give up.

Yet, what is challenging for parents as they prepare for their child is challenging for each of us as we prepare for the Christ child. The greater the sacrifices that we are willing to make, through examining our consciences, confessing our sins, and accepting the grace of reconciliation, the greater the joy that we will be open to throughout the entire Christmas Season and throughout this new year of grace.

My sisters and brothers, we are called to be witnesses that God has touched our lives and has come expressly for the salvation of our world. The call of salvation is here in our midst. Let us live in faith and confidence. God will complete His work. And, let us live our lives in this Advent season and beyond in a way as to more fruitfully receive His call.

Don't Be Afraid. Be a blessing.

He Lives in Us

Born as a child to our glorious Father God
We walk by faith and to Him we applaud
We are blessed beyond measure as His love abounds
In His humble presence is where Christ Jesus is found
Remember to keep God first as He leads our way
Guiding us along our journey day by day
Through prayer, supplication and devoted faithfulness
Seek the Kingdom of God and a life of holiness

Self-Reflections

Use the space below to reflect on the poems in this collection in the context of your own turning points.

_____

_____

_____

_____

_____

_____

_____

_____

_____

_____

_____

_____

_____

_____

_____